THIS BOOK
BELONGS TO:

_____

Birth date:

_____

Birth time:

_____

Birth location:

_____

A.B'J

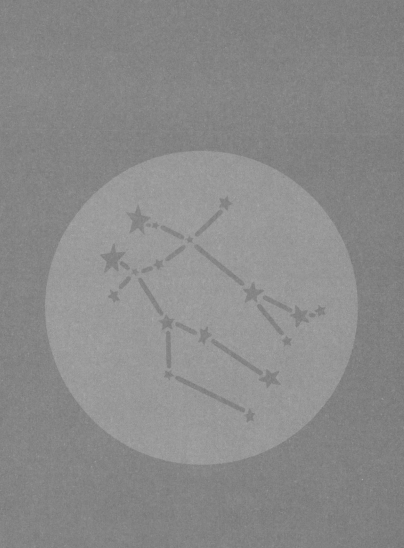

ZODIAC SIGNS

GEMINI

ZODIAC SIGNS

GEMINI

COLIN BEDELL

STERLING ETHOS
New York

STERLING ETHOS
New York

An Imprint of Sterling Publishing Co., Inc.

STERLING ETHOS and the distinctive Sterling Ethos logo are
registered trademarks of Sterling Publishing Co., Inc.

Text © 2020 Colin Bedell
Cover © 2020 Sterling Publishing Co., Inc.

ISBN 978-1-4549-3893-4

Distributed in Canada by Sterling Publishing Co., Inc.
c/o Canadian Manda Group, 664 Annette Street
Toronto, Ontario M6S 2C8, Canada
Distributed in the United Kingdom by GMC Distribution Services
Castle Place, 166 High Street, Lewes, East Sussex BN7 1XU, England
Distributed in Australia by NewSouth Books
University of New South Wales, Sydney, NSW 2052, Australia

For information about custom editions, special sales, and premium
and corporate purchases, please contact Sterling Special Sales at
800-805-5489 or specialsales@sterlingpublishing.com.

Manufactured in China

2 4 6 8 10 9 7 5 3

sterlingpublishing.com

Cover design by Elizabeth Mihaltse Lindy
Cover and endpaper illustration by Sarah Frances
Interior design by Nancy Singer
Zodiac signs © wikki33 and macrovector/freepik

To my Gemini twin Courtney
who helped me find my voice and my words.

This book uses third-person plural pronouns (they, them, their, theirs) exclusively when referring to people, either in the singular or the plural. Saying "they" instead of "he," "she," "he or she," or "he/she" is a grammatically correct way to include folks of all genders, as well as keeping the focus on the Gemini's behavior, rather than their gender. A note about Gemini and gender: In countless astrology texts, Gemini is gendered as male. That is, the pronouns "he," "him," and "his" are used to describe Gemini in his quest for achievement, as he expresses exquisite self-control. In shifting away from using gendered pronouns, I hope this book will provide more universal descriptions of the archetype in action, rather than dwelling on binary gender, which is not a useful tool for me.

CONTENTS

♊

INTRODUCTION

After the slumber of winter and in the midst of spring's full flowering, a Gemini is born. At the moment of a Gemini birth, the Sun shines behind the constellation of the Great Twins, and a soul enters the Earth armed with the knowledge of how to change a heart, which is the intelligence that can change the world.

The zodiac year begins on the spring equinox, when the universe honors Aries the Ram. This first sign in the zodiac teaches us how to explore our identity, power, divinity, passions, and lovability. Then, on April 21, Taurus the Bull gently stewards us out of Aries's Martian fire and into the Venusian Eden of aesthetics, pleasure, personal security, and clarity. Aries helps understand what follows after "I am . . . ," and Taurus places the answers to "I have . . ." in our hands and heart. On May 21, the zodiac calendar follows the first two animal signs with human twins. Building on the foundation of the Aries fire of identity and the Taurus groundedness that keeps us secure and in pleasure, Gemini points to our mind and mouth to help us answer the question, "I think . . ."

When the planets shine behind Gemini, we're all asked to think critically, exercise adaptability, sharpen our verbal communication skills, concentrate on active listening, cause a bit of friendly mischief, and—as the symbolism of the Twins teaches us—interpersonally connect with others. Those born between May 21 and June 21 and/or carrying other personal planet aspects in Gemini—from the rising to the moon, mercury, venus, and mars—are the messengers assigned to lead these crucial efforts and teach their successful application so the rest of the zodiac can learn from them.

That's likely you. If you're the one holding *Gemini* in your hands, then you likely have Gemini as your sun, moon, or rising sign. If you are a Gemini, then you probably already deduced that within each one is two. You have two power sources for the price of one. You have twice as much mental agility, speed, versatility, and skill to explore in this life than the other signs. You make life management and success look easy. Your ruling mythological story, planet, modality, and element help you fly to the heights you dream of, while you inspire others to do the same.

Many ancient cultures, from the Norse countries (named Freyr and Freyja), to Nigeria (Ibegii—the twins of joy and happiness), to Egypt (Nut and Geb), have a myth of the Great Twins, though the archetype for Gemini was largely inspired by the ancient Greeks. Twins named Castor and Pollux were born to the queen of Sparta, but Castor was fathered by a mortal while Pollux was fathered by the king of the Gods, Zeus himself. Myth tells us that these fraternal twins were inseparably loyal to each other, especially on heroic adventures searching for the Golden Fleece among carnage-ridden battlefields. Tragically, mortal Castor was lost in battle. When his immortal twin, Pollux, begged his divine father, Zeus, to reunite them, the Olympian king placed Castor and Pollux into the Gemini constellation, where they live together to this day.

I think it's important to take this myth with us throughout the rest of this book. This story is told through the lens of relationships, love, and loyalty. If Gemini is the first of two zodiac signs iconized by humans—the other being its Mercury sibling, Virgo the singular Maiden Woman—it is also crucial to hold in our heads and hearts that the first sign appears as two figures. Humanity begins with connection. Social theory reminds us that human beings are hardwired for interpersonal relationship. Couples therapist Esther Perel regularly shares that the quality of our relationships determines the quality of our lives.[1] As we'll explore later, in Chapter 6, "Gemini in Love," the Gemini archetype and function aren't just arcane knowledge, but are actual forms of energy that exist between two people, from the most casual to the most intimate of connection, when they feel seen, understood, and loved. Prioritizing relationships and engaging in the communication practices that sustain connection enhance the quality of our lives. If this connection is absent in relationships, suffering, addiction, anxiety, and depression can grow. So it's important to see the Gemini Twins as teachers of connection, as that's how they appear intentionally in the zodiac.

Every sign is ruled by a planet, which seamlessly matches the energy of the sign itself. Mercury rules both Gemini and Virgo, given their relationship to cognition, communication, transportation, technology, and active intelligence. Since Mercury is the first planet next to the Sun, it is the celestial subject of superlatives, as Mercury is the smallest, closest, quickest, and hottest planet in our solar system. This demonstrates the superlative possibilities available to Gemini, who's invited to be the quickest, funniest, most agile, most controversial, and most energetic person in whichever room, relationship, office, or campus they find themselves in.

Returning to ancient mythology, Mercury was the messenger god who flew between the highest heavens of Mount Olympus and the lowest depths of the Underworld, ushering critical information between these diametrically opposed forces, and even ferrying souls from the realm of the living to the realm of the dead. His Greek namesake, Hermes, means "persuasive tongue." While the shadow side of Gemini can manifest as a person who only wants to keep it heavenly and light-filled *or* hellish and cynical, high-minded Geminis allow themselves to soar to both the highest realms of thought that consciousness can allow, but also develop a perspective capable of discovering the deepest wisdom of heartbreak and suffering. This sophisticated ability to comprehend both extremes of human nature is inherent in Gemini's dualism. Society, on a personal and global level, fails when it can't hold space for that nuance. If Geminis are brave enough to convey the truth in these observations, then they can use their words to righteously inspire others.

One of the easiest ways to understand the dimensions of a zodiac sign is to remember that each one is a unique combination of two astrological concepts: an element and a modality. In order of appearance throughout the zodiac, the four elements are fire, earth, air, and water. Chronologically, the three modalities are cardinal, fixed, and mutable.

Gemini is the zodiac's mutable air sign. Born while spring transitions into summer, Gemini possesses the vitality of the evolution into a new season after another has come to a close. Geminis hold all of this transition's elegance, grace, and beauty in their lungs. As the first mutable sign preceding Virgo, Sagittarius, and Pisces, Gemini theoretically has a high level of psychological comfort with the in-between moments of the human experience. It teaches us to accept the painful but helpful paradoxes, juxtapositions, uncertainty, impermanence, change, and pivot points that are necessary for us to engage with in order to live a meaningful life.

The air element represents our analysis, perception, socialization, and conviction. Air signs Gemini, Libra, and Aquarius help us choose how to think, what words to use, which relationships to engage in, and to what high-minded principles we should aspire. The air signs also remind us who are we *without* principles, ideas, and philosophies. Gemini represents our first curiosities, which allow us to engage with the experiences ruled by air. As the first mutable and the first air sign in the zodiac, Gemini helps us make sense of life, the questions we ask, the words we choose to explore, and the messages we feel compelled to share as a storytelling species.

You've probably read the shallow interpretations and unnecessary—though sometimes funny!—Gemini slander all over the internet. In an effort to correct the misunderstandings on Gemini, this book explores the archetype in its many incarnations—from child to adult, parent to lover, and in daily life as well as in the world.

Up first is Gemini as a child, where we learn just how

fast a young Gemini can talk, crawl, walk, and then talk some more. From infancy to adolescence, Gemini children are two handfuls for parents. So I've included helpful suggestions on both affirmation and the right amount of discipline so Gemini understands boundaries, ethics, and follow-through from an early age.

Some Geminis do make the choice to grow up, and do it well. I cover common adult expressions of Gemini in chapter 2, and highlight areas in which Gemini has the opportunity to own moral authority in various life arenas, with cautionary tales about where they are most likely to miss the mark.

As a parent, Gemini doubles—of course—as teacher and caregiver. When they elect to provide for and guide little ones, Gemini parents come prepared for the mission with the right intellect, structure, and spontaneity that is sure to make a child's life meaningful. I outline parenting tips in chapter 3 for Gemini parents to understand their fire, earth, air, and water children, and build better family relationships.

Even this freedom-loving sign can absolutely commit to the right romantic relationship partners, and chapter 4 illuminates the Gemini heart in love. Nobody demonstrates the fact that the most important romantic and sexual organ is the mind quite like the Gemini. So I summarize the way to the Gemini's heart across all pairs of the zodiac. Don't worry—I don't believe in bad compatibility, especially with Geminis who can actively learn how to connect deeply with anyone if they so choose.

Once Geminis commit to an industry or profession that is evolving, interesting, intelligent, and of service to the collective, their work ethic shines. In the fifth chapter, I offer a list of helpful professions and industries, suggestions for finding your niche, and ideas that can aid the sometimes-indecisive Gemini walk a more helpful path toward merging their purpose with profit. From the communication industries to entrepreneurial adventures, there are few spaces where Geminis can't be of service.

At school, from early education to higher education, Geminis find a cure for their worst nightmare: boredom. With dozens of interests and curiosities, Geminis at school can enroll in the classes that answer their questions, learn from masters in the field, and join the extracurricular organization that gives them both a sense of belonging and wisdom. Chapter 6 explores educational styles that are a good fit for Geminis and higher education preferences that match their self-direction and multidimensional interests.

Little things make can make a big difference in a Gemini's life, so I've written tips in chapter 7 for Geminis' top routine, health, wellness, and spiritual practices, and organizational strategies that allow daily life to run smoothly. Here you'll learn what foods, exercise routines, and even days of the week work best for the Twins, so they can operate at peak capacity while contributing their intelligence, humor, and capacity for whip-smart analysis in wonderful ways.

The final chapter, "Gemini in the World," delves into the lives of four public figures born under the Gemini sun sign and how they expressed this archetype in their impact on the world. Though their life experiences derive from different racial, financial, gender, and sexual points of origin, the lives of these luminaries reflect consistent Gemini themes that offer not only fellow Geminis but the entire zodiac a helpful framework to fulfill their potential. In addition to Gemini people, I included some Gemini places that will help you see how this energy is everywhere.

It's my hope that this book can help all Gemini-influenced souls look at their twin ruled planets through a lens that clarifies, strengthens, and motivates them on their path toward discovering the truth of who they are, how they love, and what their function in this world really is. The Gemini soul understands Geminis' special mission, their function in the zodiac's collective, and how they can apply their natural gifts and abilities to healing the world.

There's no higher art form than living a soulful life, and astrology is a tool that all signs can learn from. The wisdom of the zodiac helps Geminis understand who they are, why they're here, who they're meant to love, and what they're astrologically ordained to do. When thinking of all the wonders that a Gemini can work in the world, it's easy to become overwhelmed and ask yourself if you can do it all. It's important to remember that the universe gave you Gemini energy, but it's equally crucial to understand that you're *meant* to be successful in its expression. It would not be reasonable to assume that you have Gemini gifts without the means to bring them to fruition. So together, let's get started.

GEMINI

as a Child

ook who's talking! Odds are, if Gemini children are in the room, it's them. Often at a precociously early age, the Gemini child learns how to use their hands for communicating even before they learn to crawl. Lovingly parented by Mercury, Gemini children are born to be messengers. The earlier Gemini children start learning how to observe, critically analyze, gather information through research, listen, and talk—the *better* for their adult development.

Whereas one twin of the Gemini child's sign is the scholar in training, the other twin is the mischief maker. This dynamic is sure to keep their parents on their toes! Gemini children love learning the reasoning behind the rules, then figuring out the loopholes in the logic to break them. With two children for the price of one, little Geminis quickly demonstrate to their parents that children need dualism to thrive. A happy Gemini child is one who experiences both familiarity and adventure, reliability and surprise, logic and the arts, disclosure and mystery, black and white and color.

The Gemini child will get themselves into a bit of trouble as they develop the skills to manage the paradox between these seemingly irreconcilable needs. I'd argue that the Gemini child doesn't mean any harm as they figure out how to allow the new and the familiar to coexist side by side. They're tasked with exploration, innovation, disruption, and change, which isn't an easy or, often, a culturally supported objective. They'll miss the mark every once in a while in an effort to find the bond between seeming opposites, inadvertently causing chaos. But don't forget that these machinations are generally not mean-spirited.

Beginning in infancy, it's very likely that the Gemini will show a special connection to Mercury-governed communication through an avid appreciation for talking, storytelling, reading, listening, or appreciating the visual arts. Within the heart of each Gemini child lies a message, and one of the most helpful acts a parent can perform is providing that child with a pen, paintbrush, or other means of sharing that message. It's equally beneficial to surround the Gemini child with masterful storytellers, from those in their own family of origin to those found in popular culture, including in literature, music, and cinema, as well as in academia. Creating this kind of environment will leave an incomparably positive impact on the Gemini child, allowing them to integrate the skills of presentation so that they, too, can become a teacher or storyteller when their time comes.

Gemini children bond most meaningfully to their family through verbal communication. Families of Gemini children will want to make their little ones happy by turning into audience, interviewer, and interviewee while talking to the Gemini child. Demonstrate to the little Gemini what it means to actively listen without interrupting, but rather with thoughtful questions, mirroring, and validation of the experiences and stories being told. The junior Gemini will learn through what's modeled by parents in dialogue and will soon apply those lessons when their age allows it. If you want to make a Gemini child happy, share some stories. From family oral histories to ghost stories to the lyrics of a song, anything that involves a plot, exciting characters, and wisdom will catch their attention. Since they're quick studies, you'll be amazed by how the Gemini child learns the art form of verbal communication. While watching other children and adults, they'll want to mirror the intelligence, creativity, and excitement they observe in conversation.

Gemini children will let their imagination enchant their life in magical ways. They can tap into fantasy, surrealism, and other planes of existence with rapid-fire speed. Gemini children will create universes entirely of their own making, and their self-directed personality enables them to express these universes without the help or permission of adults. With a hunger for information, Gemini children will allow their curiosities and adventurous longings to take them to other worlds inside their own head, and in their own life, too. Daydreaming should never be interrupted, because you never know what the Gemini child will find in the land of pure imagination and bring back to our world so desperate for enchantment.

Appropriate discipline does have a place in the home and in the Gemini child's life. When boundaries are crossed or improper choices are made, parents will want to spend time with the Gemini explaining exactly why their choice was irresponsible and why the appropriate consequence is being enforced. It might seem like the Gemini is talking back or pushing too hard, but these conversations are critical for their Mercury-ruled cognition. Geminis need to understand the reasoning, morality, and ethics behind parental discipline so they can draw lessons from their mistakes and make wiser choices in the future. Gemini children don't have to learn the "hard way" if their parents are willing to help them learn important life lessons from their own experience and share them clearly with the Gemini child.

As siblings and cousins, Gemini children will want to socialize often with their family. Even at a young age, Gemini children strive to be helpful, imaginative, joyful, and sometimes hell-raising influences on their generational cohorts. As air signs, they're born highly relational, with a precognitive knowledge of the language necessary to talk to others. So family relationships mean a great deal to this sign, since Gemini, as the Twins, is born in the energy of relationships. They'll know how to talk and listen to the words of the other children they're living with and will enjoy beginning to understand some of the interests they have in common. This process can build meaningful bonds in the Gemini's family of origin, where most children learn about emotions, communication, and other life-defining experiences.

In early education, Gemini children usually access language and speech either through a high aptitude, like an advanced reading level, or an impairment like dyslexia. These diametrically opposed reactions make sense for the divine fraternal twins. If a Gemini child's school highlights their language and speech as a strength, and then tailors their education to enhancing that proficiency, they have a head start toward winning the Pulitzer. If they need extra help in this area, this can still serve the Gemini's long-term success. If a Gemini child is aware that they have a communication issue—for example, a stutter or a speech impediment—they will become more sensitive to the outsider's plight throughout life. In the right therapeutic scenario, the Gemini will soon find the technique that helps them overcome the impairment, but the experience of being on the outside looking in will leave a permanent mark on their heart, making them more empathic toward and mindful of others.

A Gemini child is likely to have a wide range of passions and interests, so their family should help the Gemini taste-test all these intellectual cravings, while also encouraging a specialized focus on specific areas as they come of age. The Gemini child is a lifelong multidisciplinary student. As they mature, they'll find the common thread among their seemingly opposing interests, as long as they're not forced to choose or commit to one prematurely. Because of their mutable air quality and because they're ruled by Mercury, Gemini children are often self-directed in education, so fortunately all teachers and parents need to do is just listen to what's captivating them and provide the right resources to help them learn even more.

In school, the Gemini child will inevitably be scolded for talking too much. Authority figures will want to encourage and sometimes mandate a lengthy period of contemplation for Geminis, so other children can have a chance to participate. Learning to wait before talking is an annoying—but helpful—experience for the Gemini child's long-term development. Because the mind of a Gemini child moves rapidly, if they engage in contemplative activities first thing in the morning, like a mindfulness, meditation, or exercise routine, it'll enable them to let off some of their hyperactive steam. Taking some of that pressure off first thing in the morning gives them a greater ability to concentrate and contemplate throughout the day.

In adolescence, Gemini's aptitude for learning really begins to take flight. By their teen years, Geminis are most likely serving in leadership positions in extracurricular activities, dodging detention with their charm, ranking at the top of their class, and alternating between athletic responsibilities and their role as the star of the drama production. There's little they can't do, so they try it all.

Gemini youth should be celebrated for their "soft" skills of social competence and diverse curiosities. The dominant culture assumes that soft skills are easy, but as we all know, getting along well with others is tough. Gemini makes it look effortless. Highlight the specific behavior that helps Gemini connect to others, and celebrate their gifts. Your attention gives Gemini an opportunity to teach through demonstration, showing others how they do things differently. Our culture often encourages specialty, focus, and linear thinking, which feels like a straitjacket on the wings of the Gemini. Instead of trying to force them into the established way of doing things, parents of Gemini children can enable them to develop their strengths.

GEMINI

as an Adult

The section of the astrological chart associated with Gemini is adolescence. What's the state of being for the eternally youthful in adulthood? From an astrological point of view, adulthood begins during the Saturn Return, which occurs when a person is between twenty-seven and twenty-nine years old. Additionally, there's a celestial school of thought that says we shine into our sun sign throughout our thirties and midlife. This chapter will explore how Gemini maintains a youthful disposition in the years after their Saturn Return, while they simultaneously assume the responsibilities of adulthood.

The secret of the Gemini in adulthood is they don't take themselves too seriously—but they take life *very* seriously.

Adult Geminis aren't concerned about taking themselves too seriously. By maintaining an adolescent, ethereal quality, they feel they don't need to impress others by focusing too heavily on perfectionism and performance. However, if adult Geminis are unbalanced between freedom and accountability, they'll need to do some personal growth work in order to live their lives more fully.

Geminis are light on their feet because they're not weighed down by self-seriousness. They don't waste time caring about what the culture demands of them, and they're able to sidestep critics, jerks, and others filled with mean-spirited energy. The adult Gemini gets the joke. The critics and jerks are committed to misunderstanding them, so the adult Gemini can be as playful, focused, vulgar, sophisticated, creative, literal, and vulnerable as they want. Those low-level energies approach the Gemini with a foregone conclusion in mind, but Gemini doesn't need their regard and can easily ignore their judgment. Would-be antagonists who have already decided what they want to believe before they start investigating it aren't worth a Gemini's time. An adult Gemini repudiates single-minded criticism every time they bravely demonstrate the capabilities of the divine Twins within and change their mind. Every person, regardless of sun sign, is given the freedom of thought and transformation. Gemini, however, is divinely set up to be the one who initiates it.

Would I call an adult Gemini carefree? Not necessarily. Again, the adult Gemini takes life seriously. More than that, Gemini recognizes that "life" is so much bigger than the insignificant and meaningless things within their own purview. This is why they're seriously interested in "the other," the unknown, and the sunset that lies beyond their horizon.

You'll see Gemini gravitas in all their intellectual pursuits and how they apply wisdom in areas beyond the personal, like their family, friendships, and romances. In their professional lives, they work hard to be of service, along with their employers, to the outside world. It's easy to assume that we all think beyond ourselves in relationships and career, but remember: Our culture tends to give us permission to use relationships and work for personal gain only. Geminis see the transcendence in these experiences.

An adult Gemini can easily lighten up, as long as they are holding on to values in their heart that keep them fully engaged. In an interview with Oprah Winfrey, Dr. Brené Brown pointed out that wholehearted living requires clear values and convictions.[2] The adult Gemini will want to choose two to three values that are most important to them in order to make good decisions. Gemini should promote qualities like courage, integrity, connection, and creativity, combining them with their strongest personal convictions. They should also avoid becoming unhealthily attached to a specific end result.

A pitfall the adult Gemini may fall into is moving too fast, saying too much, and acting too soon without this clarity. As such a hyperactive, fast-moving, mental sign, Gemini's gifts need to be concentrated ever so slightly before this sign can become centered. I cannot encourage an adult Gemini enough to spend time contemplating what values they cherish before they make big decisions. If the decisions they'd like to make are in line with their core beliefs, excellent. The adult Gemini is on their way to flying to the peak of virtue. If not, they need to pause, reflect, and reprioritize. One of the most frequent critiques of Gemini is a lack of depth. This is common if the adult Gemini moves too quickly and can't bear to stick around long enough to acquire sufficient focus and carefully review all the details in a particular circumstance or relationship.

The adult Gemini will always want to maintain vigilant awareness of the power of their words. As the adage reminds us, great power carries great responsibility. So Geminis will want to remember that when they speak, people do listen, so they need to make sure they're choosing their words carefully. If they don't take the time to be mindful of what they're saying, Geminis can be master manipulators: emotionally violent, disruptive, and suffused with the poisonous side of the Mercury element. Given the influence of their language, they can shape others' perception of reality very powerfully. So if Geminis fail to find a positive way to direct their prodigious mental energies, they can turn toward deceit and even fraud.

Some helpful strategies to promote intellectual and vocal impulse control are a morning meditation practice and any therapeutic practice. A daily stillness exercise, like meditation, keeps fear-based, frantic thinking at bay, and introduces more mindful, tranquil energy, which can only uplift the Gemini's life. A therapeutic practice can provide the Gemini with helpful tools that prevent them from inventing stories without fact-checking them. Without that self-editing, Geminis can concoct masterful conspiracies that exist only in their own heads. They have a talent for confabulating the truth—which is the act of telling lies honestly. Since the Gemini is convinced of their own view of events, they'll believe their own conspiracies as honestly true, engage in self-deception, tell everyone else, and thereby spread false information.

In adulthood, the Gemini's adaptability, detachment, and flexibility work as their saving grace. Remember: While they're not too weighed down by self-seriousness, Gemini can use their cognition, mischief, lightheartedness, messages, and creativity to create catalysts for joy and change. In a holy book of ancient Chinese wisdom, *The Tao Te Ching*, mystic Lao Tzu wrote, "All things, including the grass and trees, are soft and pliable in life; dry and brittle in death. Stiffness is thus a companion of death; flexibility a companion of life. An army that cannot yield will be defeated. A tree that cannot bend will crack in the wind. The hard and stiff will be broken; the soft and supple will prevail."[3]

GEMINI

In the passage above, Geminis are given permission to stay flexible in pursuit of their passions and the wind beneath their winged sandals that keep them flying above "foolish consistency," a phrase immortalized by Gemini Sun Ralph Waldo Emerson, who wrote that it is "the hobgoblin of little minds, adored by little statesmen and philosophers and divines."[4] Not taking yourself seriously, but taking *life* seriously, gives you the elegance, social proficiency, and intelligence not only to keep doing what's working, but to adapt progressively with wisdom and competence when things are going awry.

The human experience is characterized by dualism and the law of opposites, so the adult Gemini's most crucial responsibility is to demonstrate to the rest of the zodiac the mind-set, language, analysis, and adaptability required to engage with contradiction. The adult Gemini's secret to this is thinking beyond themselves. By looking past the horizon, the adult Gemini teaches us the value of play, creativity, education, communication, emotionality, and relationships.

GEMINI

as a Parent

Only after thoroughly researching child psychology will the Gemini feel prepared to raise another human being. Like every arena in life, Gemini is two in one, so within every Gemini parent is a penchant for both motherhood and fatherhood as these terms are traditionally defined—an ability to lovingly say yes to their children's dreams and no to unfounded demands. Depending on the coparent, the Gemini parent will contribute to the household whatever missing element it needs to function beautifully. Whether that's more emotional support, structure, or caregiving, one of Gemini's strengths is in identifying the need and adapting to contribute it.

It's not all strategic and cerebral in the Gemini parent's household. They're just as excited to experience the joy, creativity, and play that surround child-rearing. A Gemini parent is usually thrilled to have an appropriate invitation to return to childhood by raising a child of their own. They'll love reliving the enchantment and wonder of childhood as they parent, and they'll want to share their own memories of youth with their children.

As a highly communicative sign, Gemini will teach their children how to read passionately, speak effectively, and observe mindfully. This tends to build a family culture where children feel safe talking to their parents. Gemini parents can make their relationships with their children feel very friendly, which inspires their children to share their thoughts, emotions, and fears with the Gemini parent. Since the area of Gemini is still adolescence and young adulthood, the Gemini parent won't forget the harsh realities of childhood. As a parent and an adult, Gemini knows that many things don't change, but some things do, and will listen very carefully to the wisdom of their children and understand that what they're experiencing and sharing is valid.

A possible blind spot for Gemini parents is the inevitable mess that comes from trying to raise another human being. A Gemini loves when things make sense, but sometimes people—and most especially our family—don't make sense to us. So a Gemini parent will want to exercise their curiosity and flexibility while they let their children become who they're meant to be without trying to force them to be like miniature versions of themselves. Gemini parents could be prepared with all the right tools, theories, and intellect, but life can turn a family's home upside down quickly. They'll want to avoid trying to engineer the uncertainty or risk out of their family. A Gemini parent can, instead, help their children work on resilience while they say, "I'm scared, too. But we're brave and we're going to face this anyway."

To fire sign children Aries, Leo, and Sagittarius, a Gemini parent will be a fellow troublemaker. When their passionate little children declare their "I am," "I will," or "I know" statements, respectively, the Gemini parent will produce the events and adventures that help their fire babies continue these conversations. The Gemini parent will teach fire sign children how to consider the interpersonal and relational concerns of the family and all the ways to hold the family together. The fire sign children will teach Gemini parents how to think less and do more, inspiring Geminis to lean less on theory and more on application of experience.

If an earth sign—Taurus, Virgo, or Capricorn—blooms on a Gemini family tree, a relationship dynamic involving contrast and synergy is born. When the Gemini parent marvels at how their earth sign children blend the best of head and hands, they'll do whatever they can to support their little tree huggers' dreams and visions. The Gemini parent will teach their earth babies how to think, listen, and speak in a way that furthers their ambition, so they can collaborate with others who want to see them succeed. The children will teach the Gemini parent the importance of decisiveness, structure, and follow-through in the house, so that safety, clarity, and integrity are given and received.

If another ethereal air sign is born to a Gemini, like another Gemini, a Libra, or an Aquarius, familiarity and friendship fall under one roof. The Gemini parent will encourage talking before crawling for these highly intellectual and vocal signs, which is a beautiful parent-child dynamic of shared values. The Gemini parent will help the air signs explore their curiosities and demonstrate the mental concentration required to succeed in them. The children will motivate their Gemini parent to fly even higher in communication and stay as light on their feet as possible, because their children will love to surprise them.

To water signs Cancer, Scorpio, and Pisces, a Gemini parent is a breath of fresh air. With a powerful understanding of the depths of emotion, intuition, and empathy in their children's hearts, the Gemini parent will offer them the tools for emotional regulation so their heart-centered power doesn't overwhelm their thinking. And the sea babies will teach their Gemini parent how to access their emotional intelligence. They'll bond beautifully as they try to merge the language of the head with the feelings of the heart.

A master storyteller, the Gemini parent will engage in meaningful, eventful conversations at home. They should share oral histories of the family so their children can understand their legacy. When their children hear themselves in these stories, they'll understand what it means to belong to a culture and will find their place in the family history. This understanding will be a gift to them.

A Gemini parent is intelligent and imaginative in their abilities to coparent and raise children. As a mutable air sign, they'll need to learn all the different styles of parenthood; figure out what works for them and their children; and discard whatever doesn't. This is a parent whose style won't look like the typical mother or father figure, but that's what makes their love so special.

GEMINI

in Love

et's begin this chapter on love with what a Gemini loves—definitions.

We say and write "love" often, but we do really know what it means? Dr. Brené Brown defines it this way: "We cultivate love when we allow our most vulnerable and powerful selves to be deeply seen and known, and when we honor the spiritual connection that grows from that offering with trust, respect, kindness and affection."[5]

Can a Gemini not only profess love but practice it along these lines? Of course. So can the rest of the zodiac. It's important to disclose here that I don't believe in the binary of "good" or "bad" compatibility. Like all signs, Gemini can learn how to connect to the entirety of the zodiac with the right amount of willingness, work, and understanding.

Love begins in the Gemini's life through the mind. And as Shakespeare (a Venus in Gemini) wrote, "Love looks not with the eyes, but with the mind. . . . And therefore is winged Cupid painted blind."[6]

When a Gemini feels a romantic spark, a longing, or the heat of desire, it's because their partner showcased the best of their intellect, curiosity, and verbal communication skills. Only then will the Gemini begin their initial descent from the skies that rule their sign.

When in love, the Gemini will want to honor their natural abilities to maintain a sense of wonder and to focus attention on their partners. Love survives and thrives when partners continue to pay attention to each other, and when a Gemini's in love, hardly a detail about their beloved escapes them. Their partners will relish knowing and feeling that that they're seen, cherished, and understood by their Gemini partner.

Additionally, Gemini will want to maintain their intrinsic sense of autonomy and freedom. It might seem antithetical to love, which appreciates closeness, but it's important to maintain the possession of self, for Gemini or otherwise. Without self, intimacy can become intrusion and an unhealthy codependency. As the sign of the Twins, Gemini knows when one ends and the other begins. They'll want to be as upfront as possible in the beginning stages of the relationship so their partner knows what love story they're coauthoring.

Lastly, given Gemini's social popularity, it's possible that a partner could feel intimidated or unsure of how much they matter. Tending to this is a twofold process. First of all, Gemini needs a village: They can't put all their expectations, needs, or demands on one romantic partner. Second, the Gemini should find out what their partner desires in terms of validation so that Gemini can provide it without compromising their robust social network. To ask a Gemini to give up relationships in order to provide security is a fool's errand—it will make Gemini feel resentful and insecure, and foster the kind of codependency any relationship should avoid.

Geminis look for a relationship in which commitment doesn't feel like a violation of their freedom. As the sign of dualism, Geminis hope for adventure, novelty, spontaneity, joy, education, stability, and friendship in their romance. To house all these qualities requires a delicate balancing act, but it can be done, and hopefully the result is that Gemini will be able to see their partner as both home and the unknown both comforting and exciting.

Oftentimes, Geminis can provide the exhilarating thrill of riding a wave, but not the safety of the anchor in a relationship. So the Gemini will be drawn to a partner imbued with structure, consistency, reliability, and accountability in order for the relationship dynamic to survive and thrive. Generally speaking, they'll align with a partner who's more comfortable initiating the anchor role. In the best-case scenario, Gemini will be receptive to and grateful for this security. When Geminis see mutuality as a helpful—as opposed to a restrictive—quality in the relationship, they can let the anchor partner sit back, relax, and take the lead in tending the solid ground beneath them. This builds trust and reliability. Variety and contrast keep the dynamic exciting and make the relationship a great environment for mutual growth and transformation. Also, Gemini will want to get out of their head and into their body, heart, and soul to access some of the most meaningful experiences when it comes to eroticism, intimacy, and love. This kind of grounding allows the relationship to go deeper than it normally would have, given Gemini's tendency to rely on physical senses to see and experience what the heart knows to be true in love.

Another possible blind spot for a Gemini in love is their tendency to interpret the worth of their partner by the words they say. It's critical for the Gemini to remember the so-called Mehrabian rule and understand that language, their specialty, is only around 7 percent of the entire communication continuum. The rest is all in the body language, tones, social cues, and seemingly limitless number of non-verbal messages being broadcast in the invisible ether. So to gain the most holistic understanding of who their partner is, Geminis need to expand their perception to hold space for everything that's being communicated nonverbally. They need to work hard to master fluency in this language, too.

As noted previously, I don't believe in inherently good or bad compatibility, because the nature of relationships is in managing complementarities and the paradox of love and desire. I've outlined below all matches Gemini can have with other signs in the zodiac, informed by the research conducted by couples therapist Esther Perel in her book *Mating in Captivity: Unlocking Erotic Intelligence* (Harper, 2017). Perel argues that love and desire are separate entities that can be reconciled carefully in romantic relationships.

As in Dr. Brown's definition of love, the roots by which love grows need to be tended with closeness, affection, warmth, understanding, and safety for them to thrive. Maintaining sexual desire requires the complete opposite, as its power is born of distance, mystery, longing, intrigue, and adventure. It's a good thing that Gemini, as the sign of sophisticated dual thinking and paradox management, can hold these two energies in harmony without choosing one or the other as more valid for relationship health. It doesn't have to be either/or when both/and is available!

GEMINI & ARIES

Between Gemini's air and Aries's fire, this is a match that is romantic, friendly, and lights up each other's lives immediately. When Gemini and Aries become romantically involved, it's entertaining, passionate, and supportive. This pair can blend the best of both affectionate love and exciting desire. Still, it'll be hard, and this speed-loving match will want to pace themselves appropriately so as not to burn out the excitement too soon. Since these signs are known for relatively short attention spans, it will keep the couple longing for each other. Aries's cardinal fire leadership skills will help Gemini focus all their energy in powerful places, and Aries will take the Mars-ruled action inspired by Gemini's Mercury-ruled ideas. Gemini will help Aries work on their impulse control and carefully consider their words or actions before speaking or acting.

GEMINI & TAURUS

When the Gemini Twins hop on to ride sweet Taurus into their Venus-ruled romantic garden, an unlikely love affair begins. This dynamic often has a wonderful sense of fondness, admiration, and wonder for each other. As a match between Gemini's mutable air and Taurus's fixed earth sign, it's a friendly competition between preservation and progress. This neighboring match has the right amount of contrast to keep the spark alive. It'll require a comprehensive conversation on how they understand and practice love, however. Gemini must learn the high art of follow-through and focus from their Taurus lover, whose concentration levels are second to none. Gentle Taurus will need to learn how to become more flexible as Gemini teaches Taurus how to navigate risk, uncertainty, and discomfort.

GEMINI & GEMINI

If there's two for the price of one in every Gemini, I hope four isn't a crowd in this pair! When Gemini falls in love with another Gemini, the enthusiasm, vitality, and adventure between them keep this more detached sign closely held in each other's embrace. The connection thrives in conversation. While they're all there, it's important to disclose what love means to each and then get to it. Given their hunger for information, they'll want to reveal their respective worlds slowly, because desire needs mystery to maintain its spark. In this same-sign match, both partners will bolster what comes to Gemini naturally in love, like friendly mischief, curiosity, conversation, and spontaneity. To sustain this powerful dynamic, they'll want to join forces to create a structure of consistency, affection, and trust, which will strengthen the pair.

GEMINI & CANCER

It's a match of the head and the heart! As two neighboring signs, cardinal water Cancer and mutable air Gemini offer the best of the Mercury-ruled head and moonlit heart in this relationship. What possibly started as a connection grounded in mild annoyance and intrigue turned into a power couple. As a tag team, know that the affection and the power of love is Cancer's domain, whereas novelty and the mystery of desire is all Gemini. It'll be a delicate step up, step back waltz, but if you see it as the key to unlocking relationship success, you'll be happy to do it. Gemini will learn the language and experience of the emotional realm from Cancer, which helps Gemini transcend the rational world they love so much. Cancer will learn logic and emotional regulation, which will help them retain their power and succeed with Gemini by their side.

GEMINI & LEO

If larger-than-life is your favorite size, this match is a perfect fit. As two generative, dynamic signs, the fixed fire Leo and the mutable air Gemini can create an exciting life together, full of affection and adventure. Ruled by the Sun, Leo infuses a great deal of warmth, power, and excitement into the Mercury-ruled curiosities of Gemini. For the foundation of love to be secure between the zodiac's Royal and the Jester, Gemini will want to give the Leo extra-special attention and affection. However, Gemini's inherent need for privacy and mystery requires breathing room, which the Leo will want to step outside of their castle comfort zone to deliver, because space protects their shared passion. For this union to function successfully, Gemini will learn more about creativity, confidence, and courage, and Leo will need to develop relational skills to make others feel included and understood.

GEMINI & VIRGO

Nerd alert! You two brainiacs are a cerebral pair, enchanted by an intellectually stimulating love. In fellow mutable earth and Mercury-ruled sign Virgo, Gemini finds a partner who's a mental match and performs the ultimate magic trick: holding their attention. In Gemini, Virgo's disarmed by a sophisticated ability to think deeply and optimistically.

Whoever's more comfortable with emotion will take the lead in building a home for love and affection here, whereas whoever's more comfortable with intrigue, uncertainty, and risk will coach the other on seduction and desire. In this connection, Gemini concentrates and commits to specific life and relationship strategies that Virgo will help them specialize in. Meanwhile, Virgo will watch and learn from Gemini in exercising their innovation, creativity, and ability to embrace imperfection.

GEMINI & LIBRA

Love's in the air! When two air signs align in a match, it's harmonious, comfortable, and pleasurable. Ruled by Venus, Libra, as a cardinal air sign, has social and artistic skills supreme enough to catch the Gemini's attention. In Mercury-ruled, mutable air Gemini, the elegant Libra finds another smooth talker whose passion for play turns this indecisive sign into one who's utterly committed. Love is Libra's domain, so they'll want to initiate the dialogue on love as practice for clear communication, which leads to inspired action. Desire is Gemini's bailiwick, so the Gemini will want to make the familiar unfamiliar—and more physical. Gemini will learn the Libra balance of emotion with intellect and how to navigate social spaces more elegantly. Libra will learn how to overcome the disease to people-please with the direct Gemini.

GEMINI & SCORPIO

This match can be a bit of heaven and Armageddon. In Pluto-ruled and fixed water-governed Scorpio, Gemini falls in love with a partner who's psychology runs the deepest. In Mercury-ruled and mutable air-influenced Gemini, Scorpio finds an imaginative and intelligent lover who keeps the match passionate and educational. The differences between them can create hellish circumstances without flexibility, however, which is why Gemini's assigned the task of providing love and affection. Scorpio has a penchant for seduction and desire, so they'll keep the mystery alive, since they don't like revealing anything. Gemini will learn how to receive, observe, and feel more deeply without an attachment to the intellectual world. Scorpio will work on adaptability and how to leave the devil they know for the angel in the unknown.

GEMINI & SAGITTARIUS

Opposites attract! These two are opposing sides of the same axis, but they have more in common than meets the uninitiated eye. Jupiter-ruled and fellow mutable fire sign Sagittarius loves to ferret out the wisdom in the data that Mercury-governed Gemini finds in their airy research. Sparks fly in this match, because it's complementary, intellectual, and passionate. Sagittarius will know how to keep the seduction alive, as they're more freedom-loving and space-needing than Gemini. Meanwhile, Gemini will coach Sagittarius on the proximity, affection, and stability that love needs to emerge. Gemini will learn how to use fewer words and more wisdom from Sagittarius, whereas Sagittarius will learn how to infuse more compassion and curiosity into their lives from the relational Twins.

GEMINI & CAPRICORN

Meet 'em at the top! This match between ethereal Gemini and mountain-climbing Capricorn is highly visionary, as they connect where the mountain meets sky. In cardinal Earth- and Saturn-ruled Capricorn, Gemini's impressed by the stature and moral authority of this dutiful sign. Capricorn slowly finds that the Mercury-ruled Gemini has more than jokes up their sleeve, but critical thinking, too. Love and affection would be Capricorn's mission to demonstrate here, as the love between these signs needs consistency, structure, and trust. For the desire to stay seductive and passionate, Gemini will want to keep the mystery, play, and seduction in the relationship. Gemini will be inspired to emulate Capricorn's morality and long-distance dream planning. From Gemini, strict Capricorn will learn how to lighten up and enjoy the pleasures of life.

GEMINI & AQUARIUS

Put it in writing! An exciting match between two air signs, Aquarius and Gemini will never run out of things to talk about or stories to write in a love letter. Ruled by innovating Uranus and with a fixed air heart, Aquarius loves to ask Gemini, "Have you thought about this?" Mercury-governed with a mutable air heart, Gemini has a love that soars when it encounters the brilliant and disruptive cognition of Aquarius. With their relational skills, Gemini will want to take the lead on the structure and reliability that love needs to breathe. Aquarius loves the unknown, so they'll teach Gemini all about longing, seduction, and desire. Gemini will learn how to stay true to their convictions more from the principled Aquarian, and Gemini will teach Aquarius how to disagree without dogma or divisiveness.

GEMINI & PISCES

Two fish in every Pisces, and two people in every Gemini. In this dualistic match, contrast, change, and novelty uplift and secure the couple. Neptune-ruled and fellow mutable sign Pisces brings to the relationship creative, empathic, and healing skills that inspire Gemini. Pisces is charmed by Gemini's Mercury intellect and mutable air communication skills. Gemini also helps Pisces look on the brighter side when Pisces becomes too bogged down in introspection. Gemini will want to facilitate conversations on how love needs the structure of consistency and reliability. Because Pisces's natural self is so mysterious to Gemini, they'll preserve the passion of this relationship as they strive to learn more and more about each other. Gemini will evolve in their nonverbal fluency and how to read a room, as instructed by Pisces, who will conversely learn the value of straight talk for clear understanding.

Now that we have reviewed all the matches in the zodiac, let's begin the ending of this chapter with how it opened. Dr. Brown wrote on love, "Shame, blame, disrespect, betrayal, and the withholding of affection damage the roots from which love grows. Love can only survive these injuries if they are acknowledged, healed and rare."[7] How can Gemini best acknowledge these injuries through their governing practice of verbal communication when they are upset with their romantic partner?

When we talk about love, it's crucial that we also talk about how to help love survive injuries through acknowledgment and healing. In other words, we can't talk about love without talking about how to apologize. Given Gemini's imperfect state of being, they'll make mistakes. We all do. So let's explore leading ideas on apologies and forgiveness so Gemini has the emotional strength to acknowledge an upset and take steps toward healing the wound.

GEMINI

A very helpful method for navigating such situations is nonviolent communication (NVC). A system invented by Dr. Marshall Rosenberg, NVC encompasses four steps not just for the Gemini who loves a framework, but for all us. The first step is observation—where the Gemini is encouraged to describe what they observed neutrally and without interpretation. The second step is the emotion that the Gemini feels when they observed the behavior from their partner. It could sound like this: "I noticed that when you walked into the room without saying hello, I felt upset . . ." The third step is identifying the need. So the Gemini will want to identity what they need from their partner. In continuing this example, the Gemini can say, "I need to feel that you see me; otherwise, I feel like I don't matter to you." And the last step is the request. The Gemini can request what they need specifically to not feel disregarded: "So when you walk in next time, can you greet me, and give me a few minutes of your time, so I can feel more connected to you?" It's important to provide the recipe for success to our partners when it comes to connection. The four steps, again, are: observation, feeling, need, and request. This is especially useful for the Gemini, but can be applied to all relationships.

I spoke with another Gemini Sun recently. Without even asking him directly what Gemini can do to improve the quality of their relationships, he said, "All a Gemini has to do is say, 'I'm sorry.' Period." He's right. As a highly intellectual sign, when Gemini hears that their behavior caused pain, they'll often run into explaining it away to the person who's experiencing the upset. That's generally the last thing the upset party needs from Gemini—more of their words. When my Gemini friend mentioned the need for an apology, I knew I needed to explore how to properly apologize.

Dr. Harriet Lerner is a Sagittarius Sun—Gemini's polar opposite sign, which has perfect vision on them, since they're across from each other on the zodiac—and a clinical psychologist who specializes in improving family and work relationships and methods for apology. Not only do many of us avoid apologizing, but we assume that we're born knowing how to do it. Dr. Lerner's techniques include avoiding add-ons to our apologies like, "I'm sorry *if*" or "I'm sorry *but*." In an interview with *Forbes* magazine, Dr. Lerner said, "High-stakes situations call for an apology that's a long-distance run—where we open our heart and listen to the feelings of the hurt party on more than one occasion." What Gemini stands to learn is that there's nothing more precious to the upset party than their gift of whole-hearted listening to the kind of anger and pain they're being accused of causing without defense, justification, or explanation. The upset speaker wants to know that the Gemini listened carefully to their feelings, validated their reality, feels genuine remorse, is willing to carry some of the pain, and is committed to avoiding an encore of the behavior that caused the upset.

I'm of the opinion that astrology can strengthen our relational intelligence and skills. With ethical understanding, your Gemini selfhood can be improved through the context of your relationship with others. It's important to remember that one sign cannot exist properly without the other. That's why the symbol of the zodiac is a circle, because each sign has a responsibility to the other, a continuity and a belonging. Each sign offers something special to Gemini, and Gemini offers something meaningful to all twelve signs.

GEMINI

at Work

I t can never be the same day twice for Gemini on the job! With vitality for variety and a gift of gab, Gemini needs a career where they can put their intellectual skills to work in industries that celebrate innovation and change. As a sign governed by Mercury, which rules the media, communication fields, technology, commerce, education, and transportation, Gemini needs to interact with others and especially appreciates using modern technology to send the messages they were born to deliver. On the job, Gemini is a student and a teacher. Whatever they know, they share. What they want to know, they ask. Along with their prodigious social skills, Gemini can uplift the bonds among coworkers through facilitating conversations and thereby promoting collaboration.

In any communication industry, Gemini can research, analyze, speak, and write because they know the power of the word. From editor to journalist, commentator, and author, Gemini can use their versatility and language skills at work with ease and to great success. Think of the works of Gemini wordsmiths like Anne Frank, Walt Whitman, and Nikki Giovanni. As student and teacher, Gemini thrives on self-directed education and finds it essential for their professional trajectory. Their work will benefit tremendously if they keep researching, learning, and attending professional events, like industry-related conferences, where they can stay current on all the latest research and theory. That way, Gemini's flexibility can move their industry toward innovation, progress, and the culture of the future.

You'll definitely find many a Gemini in Silicon Valley and other tech hubs, as Gemini is adept at using technology as a problem solver. The inventor of the World Wide Web, Sir Timothy Berners-Lee, is a Gemini. Naturally! Given their bright-eyed, alternative-possibility-loving, and yet highly mechanistic way of thinking, you can find Geminis in cutting-edge technology spaces in a range of industries, from health care to entertainment, transportation, and education. What makes the Gemini special in these spaces is their ability to humanize technology and remember how it serves people, and not the other way around. If Gemini blends the best of relational with technological in these industries, they can be among the most valuable employees on the job.

In any kind of sales or commerce field, Gemini can sell just about anything. Using their Mercurial persuasive tongue and (hopefully) nonmanipulative strategies, they can help consumers understand why their product fits the consumers' need. Within each Gemini mind is a public relations expert, copy editor, marketer, and strategist. They can utilize this range of skills to understand what the market needs, how to tell the story, and who to tell it to. Sales is another area where relational skills are essential for the bottom line, and it's Gemini's ease in communication, and perhaps their popularity, that makes them shine in this role.

In education, a Gemini can find a professional sanctuary. From kindergarten teacher to college professor teaching graduate students, a Gemini academic, with their adaptable intelligence, can figure out what each student needs to learn effectively. Based on their ability to think, speak, and listen in diverse settings, they know how to individualize the teaching styles and curriculum to fit the students' most effective mode of learning. Geminis love the magic that happens between teacher and student as they alternate roles and explore, disagree, validate, and expand on preexisting theory together.

Now that we covered how Gemini uses their intellect in communication, tech, commerce, and education, let us review the deeper, more universal meaning of why they feel compelled to contribute to a range of industries. Gemini has an obligation to harness their intelligence in an effort to heal others. According to the solar chart, Gemini is situated at the first house of identity, which then makes Pisces the ruler of their tenth house of career. This placement means that Pisces's creative sensibilities, artistry, and soulful approach to life's trajectory extend to the Gemini's career.

It's too simplistic to just connect Gemini's career path to how smart and communicative they can be. Given Gemini's mutable energy, they can contribute a range of skills and styles to their career beyond just intellect and language. Gemini has to blend the mental and emotional with inspirational Pisces, inspiring their highest mission.

The mutable receptivity of both Gemini and Pisces means that it's important for Geminis to spend enough time in contemplation so they can identify the deeply held personal beliefs behind their choice of career. The Twins have an open mind, so they can almost be easily persuaded to pursue inauthentic and ultimately unimportant paths if they're not following their own genuine personal convictions. Their career path might be completely traditional, nontraditional, or a combination of the two. To know which one is in alignment with their truest self, Geminis need to spend time alone to think. Then they'll know how their gifts and abilities could best contribute to compassionate healing.

Since we covered a great deal of what Gemini does well on the job, let's discuss where they have opportunities for growth. First, with all their Mercurial energy, it's difficult for Gemini to focus on one thing at a time because they can multitask like magic. However, there's a time and a place for their multitasking and for concentration. In order for Geminis to be all they can be on the job, it's crucial for them to finish what they start, own what they can't, or delegate it to someone else if they can't undertake it themselves. One of the most difficult scarlet letters to wash off at work is a reputation for unreliability or inconsistency. Unfortunately,

Geminis can fall into those habits if they're not carefully concentrating on or committed to the completion of a task.

Gemini is smart enough to know when they're distracted, instead of focused. That's why it's especially important for them to enforce mental boundaries on the job so as not to interrupt their work flow. Whether that means blocking social media sites on the internet browser or moving the phone far enough away not to read unrelated texts, a few preventive measures go a long way. Given Gemini's ability to do it all at once, another helpful habit for Gemini is asking whether or not a particular task is a time-sensitive priority. Since they're so fast and so agile, they can work well under pressure, assuming they know what tasks need to be completed more urgently and which they can put on the back burner.

Gemini will want to ask supervisors and colleagues, "What's the time line on this? What needs to be done by when?" This helps them understand the expectations at hand. From there, Gemini can agree, negotiate, delegate, or refuse the assignment, based on their skills, current workload, and projected turnaround time. Having straightforward conversations at work is hard, but they're necessary to develop trust among colleagues. Gemini's honesty, clear communication, and questioning identify them as reliable because their cognition is so focused; they can prioritize specific tasks, helping them deliver on those expectations.

Another skill Gemini will want to pick up on at work is the ability to see, hear, and feel with their inner senses. As mentioned, Gemini's verbal fluency is top-notch. What they need to practice is listening to the nonverbal—and there's no place like work to practice how moods, subtexts, body language, and cues can really tell a story. So for Gemini to acclimate and adapt to their work culture, they'll want to honor their language skills while practicing hard at seeing, hearing, and feeling all the things that aren't being said. It's Gemini's responsibility to identify what's *not* being said and apply language to it at work. It could begin as simply as this: "Hey, [insert colleague name here], I noticed in the meeting that your body language shifted a bit when I presented and shared my idea. I don't want to make any assumptions, but is there something we need to clear up?"

Utilizing the best of their emotional and intellectual communication skills, Gemini can proactively defuse any possible miscommunications. It's not easy to see the future, but Gemini's mind can come close to anticipating possible professional pitfalls if they're willing and brave enough to step in with strong communication after observing colleagues' emotional discomfort. We're living in a time when it's no longer just the bottom line that's a nonnegotiable, but also the employee's relational intelligence. So Gemini will want to showcase the best of their mind and heart on the job.

Last but not least: listening. Just because Gemini is ready to talk does not mean their colleagues are ready to listen. A Gemini will want to make sure the environment is right for discussion by beginning with a few polite bids for their fellow employee's attention. Gemini can start by saying, "Hi, [Name], I had an idea I want to run past you. Do you have about ten minutes so I can review this with you?" If they say no, Gemini will want to ask when they'll have time, and then follow up later on to confirm.

When Gemini's the listener and not the speaker, the most effective way to ensure accuracy in the dialogue is to mirror back. It'll seem a little clunky at first, but you might as well lean into this discomfort before the error is made. Gemini can say, "Let me make sure I understood you. So you want me to [identify the task and action] by [date and time]? Did I get that right?" This is essential, because studies on listening show that we often have a 13 percent accuracy rate, which means we miss 87 percent of vital information. This mirroring exercise increases our accuracy and efficiency. If it is done well, the speaker will confirm. If not, hopefully they'll clarify. You'd be amazed at how kindly people take to Gemini when they showcase the best of their cognition, listening, and language skills with these techniques.

Pisces, as the ruler of Gemini's career, imbues Gemini with a soulful professional mission. If Gemini sees their work as a ministry that comforts the afflicted and disrupts the comfortable, they will be successful professionally. Geminis measure their professional value by asking themselves, "Did I do my part to make people feel seen, heard, and understood? Did I listen carefully and not interrupt?" If the answer is yes, the Gemini constellation will shine even brighter in their honor. If not, it's never too late to start again.

GEMINI

in School

E ver the intellectual, Gemini thrives in academic spaces. From primary school to higher education, only within schools and on campuses can the curious Gemini find the means to unlock other worlds. Ruled by the exceptionally intelligent Mercury, school-going Gemini is obligated to mindfully pay attention, analyze, listen, communicate, read, and write . . . but also to engage in a bit of mischief. There's no place on Earth quite like school for Gemini to contribute their Mercury-ruled power.

EARLY EDUCATION

As a child in school, Gemini will learn by talking ideas and subjects out with their teachers. They're simultaneously independent and collaborative students, though I'd argue that the younger Gemini needs as much collaboration to discuss what they're thinking as possible. A curious and creative thinker, Gemini will need to investigate their passions. They are self-starters in that way, but a young Gemini will appreciate an adult's help to clarify their ideas.

As far as favorite subjects are concerned, no two Geminis are alike, because each one is two different personalities competing for airtime, but the language arts, the humanities, and the arts is often where they shine. Any subject with a story line hooks the Twins. So if a Gemini is struggling with a particular subject, like math, have the Gemini focus on the word problems to bolster their confidence in the subject, which encourages them to wrap their head around numbers.

In early childhood, and especially in school, parents will want to help the Gemini feel empowered in their relationships. Encourage your Gemini student to foster positive connections with other children, help them take a stand against bullying, and talk through other potentially traumatizing experiences that can scar children at an early age. Since Gemini has the mind and mouth to seek kindness, compassion, and fairness, other children will listen to their ideas and follow their example. In the same way, when Gemini makes the choice to mock a fellow student, others may follow suit, which can be a problem. Given Gemini's fascination with friendly mischief, the parent of a Gemini would be wise to help them understand the difference between fun and making fun of others at their expense.

Of course, it's never too early to speak to the Gemini student about managing their appetite for disruption, distraction, and talking too much. They don't mean undermine the educational environment, but they have limitless quicksilver energy that can overwhelm them in youth. Teachers and parents of Gemini students will want to encourage them to pay attention to the appropriate rules and boundaries of the classroom, and remind them to consider the length of time they talk, as opposed to listening. This is where most Gemini students incur disciplinary action. Frequently, they speak too fast, too often, and disrupt the classroom ebb and flow. So you'll want to encourage the Gemini's curiosities with the same enthusiasm as you'll want to guide the Gemini student to listen and pay attention to what's happening in the classroom before offering commentary.

MIDDLE SCHOOL AND HIGH SCHOOL

In middle school and high school, the Gemini student begins to let their relational skills really shine. As they proceed through primary school and secondary school, the Gemini student will start to connect with their classmates and teachers very meaningfully, based on how well they verbally communicate. Here teachers and parents of Gemini will want to emphasize to Gemini that their relational intelligence and communication skills are a gift. This positive affirmation won't go straight to the Gemini's ego as much as it will help the Gemini student understand that with this privilege comes the responsibility of using it well.

Authority figures will want to highlight the Gemini's social influence, popularity, and magnetism, and encourage them to use these gifts in a positive way. Gemini can be a huge help to students who aren't as comfortable in relational or communication spaces. By helping out their peers, Geminis extend their gifts and allow other students to feel seen and heard, which can be a bright light in an otherwise dark situation. All it takes is one Gemini student to say, "You can sit here" or "We haven't heard from [Name] in a moment. Is there something you'd like to share?" or "Do you want to join our group?" Comforting, inclusive language helps students who feel uninvited or not cool enough to feel that they matter. We often regret failures of kindness beyond anything else, and if a Gemini can model kindness to other students, it can have a huge impact in school.

Gemini students will likely get involved in a range of extracurricular services and leadership opportunities where they can engage with other students and be a part of something bigger than themselves. Parents will want to have the Gemini double- and triple-check their schedules, because they'll be booked and busy all week long. Gemini is talented in many things, but paying attention to time and details may sometimes be beyond them. So hopefully parental and teacher influence can help keep the Gemini student on schedule and time-managed.

That being said, it's important for Gemini to avoid last-minute completion of their work. Just because they can work faster and sometimes harder at the eleventh hour doesn't mean they should! The earlier the Gemini student learns to get a head start and do bursts of work in preparation for the homework deadline, the more meaningful their schoolwork will be. In their youthful optimism, Gemini students can overestimate how much time they have to complete assignments, so it's helpful to have authority figures encourage Geminis to maximize all the time they can.

It's totally normal for the Gemini student not to recognize what passions and subjects they like the most. They're likely proficient in a range of subjects, which makes the decision to specialize in one even more challenging. So parents and teachers will want to pay attention to what the Gemini is talking about the most. Their conversations are clues to their passions and potential career paths. As a former Gemini student myself, I'm so grateful that my parents didn't force me to make a decision too early. They let my Gemini mouth talk about mysticism, astronomy, psychology, and mythology ad infinitum. Now I do it for a living.

HIGHER EDUCATION

If the Gemini student decides that higher education is a wise choice for them—and keep in mind that it's not for everyone!—they'll thrive in a collegiate environment that is organized around research and the humanities. Of course, there will be Gemini academics who are drawn to engineering, math, and science. From medicine to architecture, their Mercurial abilities allow Gemini to contribute effectively to almost anything. The Gemini student's essential motivation—what keeps them enrolled, engaged, studying, and excelling—is fairly consistent: Will this make a difference in the lives of others? As we explored earlier on Gemini's career path, they are obligated to be of intellectual service throughout their professional lives. So it's crucial that what the Gemini learns in college allows them to do just that.

Given their airy tendencies, it's likely that the Gemini student will want to enroll in a college that's a bit far from home. Gemini is born with a hunger for information and cross-cultural experiences that extend beyond the confines of home, so they'll be quick to consider going "away" to school. If they decide to stay closer to home, because they're happy with their home environment, of course that works, too! However, Gemini may stay on campus longer than they stay home to really absorb the academic energy. In class, Gemini—if prepared!—will contribute to seminars and lectures with thoughtful analysis of the material and shift the dialogue in wonderful directions. If Gemini didn't read or complete the work because they were too busy socializing, they'll probably give such a convincing anecdote in the lecture that the class will be none the wiser.

As a college roommate, Gemini will use their relational curiosity to increase camaraderie in shared social spaces. Hopefully, they'll lean on their Mercury talents to take the time to understand and get to know the people they're living with. Sooner rather than later, wherever the Gemini is living becomes a social hub. This is fantastic for networking, collaboration, and the memories that come to define an educational experience. Not so great if the Gemini is living with more introverted individuals who need time to decompress in solitude. The Gemini freshman is encouraged to gauge the temperature of the people they've living with and find out their boundaries and expectations when it comes to quiet time for homework, bedtime, curfew, socializing, and parties, so everyone's in agreement throughout the academic year.

Just as in middle school and high school, Gemini students would be wise not to commit to a major or a career too soon, since they'll change their mind many, many times every semester. Wrestling with some uncertainty is the price of admission for first- and second-year students in college, so Gemini will want to stay comfortable with saying, "I don't know what I want to do yet, but I'm having fun studying all the subjects I'm passionate about!" If Gemini is still unsure about their favorite by their junior year, I'd encourage them to dive deeper into literature, the humanities, and psychology. Gemini wings can fly at full span when they're reading, analyzing, and communicating in these disciplines. I'd argue that this point in higher education is where the moment arrives that confirms the cumulative passions of the Gemini's life. They'll realize why they were curious about all these seemingly disparate topics and find the book, the system, or the idea that merges them all into one comprehensive wholeness.

If they're still struggling with uncertainty, a gap year or a study-abroad program could reinvigorate the Gemini student's curiosity. Though most students are not encouraged to take time off or explore other places, Geminis, in particular, should be prompted to do so. Gemini should know as early as possible that their personal, educational, and professional paths are never going to look like everyone else's. If Gemini can follow their heart and mind without worrying about what they're "supposed" to do, they'll always carry that fearlessness and all the knowledge they'll acquire on their travels within their heart.

When it finally comes time to graduate, the Gemini student will walk across that commencement stage and understand how every bizarre curiosity, rejection, and adventure took them there. More than most sun signs, Gemini has a deeply meaningful attachment to academics, and earning that degree will be especially significant for them. If, after they receive their undergraduate degree, they're called to return to school, they should do it. Mercury chose Gemini and Virgo for a reason to excel in educational spaces, so while some signs aren't tuned in to the specific frequency of graduate or even doctoral education, Gemini certainly is. Even though the financial and personal costs associated with graduate education can be extremely high, the rewards will be great. When Gemini becomes the moral authority in their field and can speak and teach from expertise, they will experience great pride in knowing that people are listening carefully to their eloquence, and that they are using their gifts to make a difference in other's lives.

7

GEMINI

in Daily Life

I f any sign needs to know that little things make a big difference, it's Gemini. Often they're analyzing, moving, or speaking too fast to stop and register the divine in the details. If they can zoom in as well as they can zoom out in day-to-day experiences, Gemini will be unstoppable in their daily life. In this chapter, we'll first offer an overview of Gemini in relation to the body, and then tackle the personal growth strategies that can improve a Gemini's routine, health, and wellness.

Let's discuss which parts of the body Gemini rules; this includes the shoulders, lungs, arms, hands, and fingers. Gemini, as the sign of duality, demonstrates the dual nature of these body parts: two of each, carefully balanced down the middle.

On to the morning sunrise. The moment the Gemini's winged feet touch solid ground after gliding out of a night's sleep, they should not reach for their phone. Given Gemini's relationship to the higher mind, one of the most powerful choices a Gemini can make in the morning is devoting at least an hour of mental stillness with a contemplation, prayer, or meditation exercise. Geminis don't need to meditate for the entire hour, but they do need that block of time to align with tranquility. Our minds are most impressionable and receptive to new ideas first thing in the morning. So rather than taking on the frenzy of social media and the news right away, the Gemini needs to make sure the first messages they receive are peaceful, focused, and clarifying. This can make a huge impact on them throughout the day.

A disciplined meditation practice, like transcendental meditation, or even five minutes spent monitoring the breath first thing in the morning will positively influence almost every arena the Gemini finds themselves in. Study after study consistently proves that meditation improves concentration, efficiency, and quality of life. It's free and you can do it anytime, anywhere. So why not use this ancient self-care strategy that bolsters the strength of the Gemini mind? In addition, since Gemini rules the lungs, the Gemini needs to pay attention to their breath. They'll want to find the emotional patterns connected to what they're doing while exhaling and inhaling. When they're stressed, Gemini can always come back to the breath and honor their element of air, which is keeping them alive, but can also regulate the emotions.

As far as physical exercise is concerned, any movement that is cardiovascular and boosts the Gemini's ability to stay agile, like running or swimming, could really help them let off some of that Mercury steam. If possible, some stretching exercises and embodiment practices will allow the Gemini to stay present in the body as much as they exist in the mental realm. There's no preferred time for physical exercise, unlike a meditation practice first thing in the morning, but a Gemini should exercise as often as possible.

If Gemini can blend the best of a mental and physical routine, they'll ground themselves before the chaos of the day begins with the right attitude to handle whatever comes their way. They can only engage in the consumption of energy from other people—through their phones or otherwise—after they've first given to themselves. So many Geminis rely on spoken or written language that it's important for them to center themselves in clarity and understanding before the people who lean on their wisdom receive it.

In terms of nutrition, Gemini likes their meals light and breezy. I would never call Gemini a foodie. It's not that they don't like food, though they're much more concerned with other details and arenas of life. For breakfast, a Gemini needs whatever's healthy, quick, and easily eaten on the go. Nutritious smoothies, fruit, nuts, and portable coffee are all good options. Breakfast, for them, doesn't have to be an all-encompassing experience. It just needs to be efficient and delicious. The same can be said for lunch and dinner. As long as there's variety and Gemini isn't weighed down by their food, they'll eat it. Gemini should eat foods that bolster their cognitive function, like leafy green vegetables, fatty fish, walnuts, and berries. These foods have high nutritional value but low density. That's what the Gemini is looking for in a meal.

Since Gemini rules the lungs, Gemini would be smart not to pick up smoking as a habit or indulge in any substance that diminishes their capacity to breathe. They rely on their respiratory system to engage in their most valued activities: They need their air to think, speak, and move efficiently. The cleanest atmosphere is ideal for Gemini, as well as the best air quality. A dehumidifier and other air sanitation solutions, like smudging, can give Gemini the extra boost they need.

Always inspired by self-expression, fashion is another language the Gemini speaks fluently. Gemini loves to merge high and low fashion by pairing more sophisticated styles with casual accessories. Think a blazer or pencil skirt with sneakers. Gemini has a wonderful time exploring where downtown and uptown meet on the body. The two Twins in each Gemini love to nod to more classic and timeless styles that never go out of fashion, while still keeping tabs on what's new and exciting—Gemini will always stay on trend by wearing the colors, patterns, and textures that are celebrated each season. It's important for the Gemini to wear material that doesn't restrict their movement. Light, ethereal, and sometimes oversized garments suit the Gemini who doesn't want to be too tailored and constricted in their outfits. Given their passion for reinvention, Gemini may look drastically different each time you see them. They love to explore new colors and loud patterns, as well as different hairstyles and accessories.

With their ethereal soul, Gemini can live almost any-where, though they tend to find greater success in fast-paced urban areas. Gemini is comfortable with the speed of city life. The metropolis is Gemini's mecca, where they're hardly limited in terms of what museum, boutique, restaurant, theater, or park to choose. They can partici-pate in one of their favorite hobbies in cities, too—people watching! Gemini is so curious and will enjoy trying to understand a wide range of people. In a diverse environ-ment, Gemini is never bored, and is always a step away from a chance encounter with strangers. At the same time, we have to honor the more contemplative twin. So, if the Gemini decides to live in a city, they'll also need tranquil time away to reconnect with nature. Think of Gemini Sun Henry David Thoreau, a transcendentalist who contem-plated some of life's most difficult complexities while sur-rounded by nature on Walden Pond. Still, if a Gemini lives in a calmer environment, like the country or the suburbs, their adventure-craving other half will have to be honored in some way. Short getaway trips are perfect for the coun-try-Gemini to leave the comforts of home and experience new places, even just for a short time. That way, the Twins' needs for both stability and adventure are met seamlessly.

As previously discussed, Pisces is the ruler of Gemini's career sector, which impels them to see their career through a healing lens. Similarly, Scorpio is the ruler of Gemini's day-to-day activity, which propels them to operate at peak capacity. Scorpio governs the inner mind, the mysteries of the subconscious, and the dangers of human existence. With this in mind, I highly encourage Gemini to either self-research psychological modalities or consider consulting a therapist. Gemini needs a safe space to explore the darker recesses of the human mind—the shadow, ego, and trauma—since Scorpio rules this area. Meeting with a mental health professional will provide Gemini with objective instruction that will help them sift through their life experiences and develop the tools for shame resilience and relational health.

The Gemini can outsmart family, friends, and lovers, but they can't cast a spell on a therapist who's trained to find patterns, defense mechanisms, and other ways that Gemini, like all of us, self-sabotages. Gemini will be challenged and empowered by having an objective and highly educated mental health professional guide them toward managing their contrasting personalities, adaptability, and more. With the right therapist, the Gemini will develop a good measure of self-acceptance and emotional wellness that allows them to be their controversial, disruptive, and intelligent selves.

Additionally, with Gemini leaning on a therapist they can transfer what they learn from this healing space to their family and careers. Remember: Gemini is hardwired to be of service. So when they cultivate resilience in response to their own shame, address their suffering, and learn how to manage discomfort, they become the most qualified wayshowers for others. Navigating through our own pain operates like X-ray vision, enabling us to see the pain of others. When Geminis work on their personal development, they gain the ability to help others and express their need to offer service within integrity.

Though surviving on only a few hours of sleep has become a perverse badge of honor in contemporary society, Geminis need their slumber. The way they use their mind and intelligence all day demands a healthy amount of sleep. If Gemini meditated in the morning, exercised throughout the day, and contributed meaningfully to work and relationships, a natural state of sleepiness should occur. If not, breathing exercises, nighttime mediation, or even white noise can quiet the Gemini mind so they can rest their brilliant selves before sunrise.

GEMINI

in the World

One of the most helpful ways to understand how all twelve signs express themselves is by exploring past and present public figures. Of course, we need to remember that the coverage and analysis of their lives may be subjective and sensationalistic. That being said, we can still use their stories to find evidence of the many ways Gemini, in this case, expresses its power through the people born under its sign, who made and continue to make an impact on the world with their unique gifts.

There are dozens of worthy public Gemini personalities whose lives I could delve into in this chapter, and their stories would all show us how their life context validates and complicates the archetype. I chose the following four to explore: Kendrick Lamar, Marilyn Monroe, Harvey Milk, and Laverne Cox. Born in different times, and belonging to diverse classes, races, and genders, these four Geminis (or eight depending on how you examine them!) demonstrate both the tragedy and glory of living a brave life while owning your voice in the face of people who would rather not have to listen to it.

Honorable mention to diarist Anne Frank, whose words captured the fear and hope of Jews throughout World War II, as well as the Notorious B.I.G., who conveyed an emotional rawness through his lyrics on crime, violence, and romance, and placed the East Coast rappers in a place of prominence. There's also President John F. Kennedy, whose ideas on service, peace, and alternative possibilities spoke to the heart of the American people, and actress Angelina Jolie, whose star quality shows both the danger-seeking and compassion-loving needs of the Gemini.

LAVERNE COX

Laverne Cox is an Emmy Award–winning actress and activist. As Sophia Burset on the television show *Orange Is the New Black*, Laverne became the first transgender woman to be nominated for a Primetime Emmy, and she went on to win a Daytime Emmy Award for Outstanding Special Class Special as executive producer for *Laverne Cox Presents: The T Word*. Laverne's Gemini gifts shine through many modalities. Laverne's professional adaptability—actress, producer, and writer—speak to the best of the Gemini who can do it all and make it look easy.

Her educational path follows that of the evolving Gemini, too. Laverne is a graduate of the Alabama School of Fine Arts, where she majored in creative writing before committing to dance. Laverne then studied for two years at Indiana University Bloomington before transferring to Marymount Manhattan College in New York City, where she switched her passions from dancing to acting. From writing, to dance, and drama, Laverne is proficient in many creative techniques and blends the best of all of them in her work.

As an activist, Laverne Cox is lauded by her LGBTQ+ peers for being a trailblazer for the transgender community and has earned numerous awards for her activist approach in spreading awareness. Laverne's impact and prominence in the media have led to a growing conversation about transgender culture, specifically transgender women, and how being transgender intersects with one's race. Given her Gemini ability to connect meaningful points and understand nuance, Laverne is leading thoughtful, intersectional dialogue on the layers of identity in a time when culture is listening carefully.

Laverne puts her quicksilver Mercury intelligence and storytelling capabilities in service to activism and awareness in Gemini fashion. In a 2016 interview with *Marie Claire*, Laverne said, "What I'm encouraged by as an artist is that this is a time for us to express our voices even more. These moments when artists can speak truth to power mean much more now than they have. It's about us continuing to elevate truth, trying to raise people's consciousness and not trying to divide people. That's where I think the arts will help most."

Just like famous twins Mary-Kate and Ashley Olsen and Beyoncé's twins Rumi and Sir Cater, what makes Laverne very Gemini is that she's a twin and born under the sign of Gemini. Laverne and her twin brother M Lamar were born on May 29 in Mobile, Alabama. In two episodes of *Orange Is the New Black*, M Lamar portrayed Sophia Burset before her transition. Being a Gemini and a twin makes one particularly express the best of this multitalented, adaptable, and relational energy, since Gemini is born in partnership. They're immediately enrolled in the school of the interpersonal arts, and this education is readily apparent in even the most superficial interactions. If you watch Laverne's interviews alone, you immediately get a sense of her empathy, curiosity, and warmth.

In the June 2014 issue of *Time magazine*, a portrait of Laverne Cox appeared on the cover and the title read, "The Transgender Tipping Point." Laverne has used her amazing Gemini energy in service of trans representation in a way that no one has before, embodying her sign's best and strongest characteristics.

MARILYN MONROE

One name immediately calls up a legend that feels eternal: Marilyn. Born Norma Jean Mortensen in Los Angeles on June 1, 1926, Norma Jean would change her hair and become a model, singer, and Hollywood star, known as Marilyn Monroe. Performing the "blonde bombshell" persona and acting like a ditzy airhead on camera was easy for a woman of Gemini duality. Marilyn was born "the other" as Norma first. So she could easily morph into whoever the Hollywood elite desired her to be.

As such, Marilyn Monroe's ability to Gemini-mirror and reflect the changing norms and attitudes on sexuality and gender throughout the 1950s and '60s catapulted her to superstardom, and her unfinished story is still being written in the Hollywood conscience. The theories on her life and death are all so widely different that an objective viewer has to wonder how so many narratives can be based on just one subject.

Marilyn's death gave birth to as many conspiracies as did her lived experiences. This is a uniquely Gemini story. This sign's elusiveness and its ability to change quickly and mirror the needs of others gives Gemini the ability to make the audience see whatever they want to see. As an actress, Marilyn clearly knew how to play the dumb blonde—apparently so convincingly that many still believe it wasn't an act. Friends and writers, who have done significant biographical research, theorize that Marilyn was, in reality, quite intelligent, with an extensive library of classic literature and a perceptive ability so keen she pretended to be the butt of the joke . . . but the real punch line was that she was fooling others. Marilyn said, "I've never fooled anyone. I've let people fool themselves. They didn't bother to find out who and what I was. Instead they would invent a character for me. I wouldn't argue with them. They were obviously loving somebody I wasn't."

Underneath the sex appeal and glamour of Hollywood, Marilyn demonstrated Gemini's relational intelligence, compassion, and commitment to activism. A powerful example of this is Marilyn's support of Ella Fitzgerald. Ella's race and physicality were liabilities in the view of owners of the more glamorous LA nightclubs. When Marilyn learned that Ella couldn't book a performance at the famous Mocambo nightclub, she used her privilege and star quality to make space for Ella. Though Ella would not have been the first African-American to sing at the Mocambo, the club's owner felt the heavyset Fitzgerald lacked the sex appeal to draw crowds. Marilyn had an idea. If the owner booked Fitzgerald, Marilyn promised to sit at the front of the audience nightly and bring along other celebrities. The owner agreed, Ella was booked, Marilyn and other Hollywood stars were seated in the front row, and, in Ella's words, "After that, I never had to work a small jazz club ever again."

Hollywood stars have come and gone before and after Marilyn Monroe, yet only a select few secured a place for themselves as icons of popular culture, and fewer still achieved her level of stardom. What makes Marilyn's enduring legacy uniquely Geminian is the mystery that surrounds it. Was it Marilyn's charisma, intelligence, beauty, or another indescribable characteristic that placed her story in the Hollywood firmament? We still don't know. That's Gemini. That's Marilyn.

KENDRICK LAMAR

"The New King of Hip Hop," Kendrick Lamar was born in Compton, California on June 17, 1987. Raised in a musical family—his name was chosen by his mother for Sagittarius Sun Eddie Kendrick of The Temptations—Kendrick was only sixteen years old when he released his mixtape. In cheeky Gemini style, it was under a pseudonym, K-DOT. Thirteen Grammy awards, six *Billboard* awards, and even a

Pulitzer Prize later, rapper, songwriter, and producer Kendrick Lamar follows a long royal tradition of Gemini wordsmiths in music.

When he was only eight years old, he witnessed fellow Gemini Sun Tupac Shakur perform and record his video for "California Love," which initiated Kendrick into this line of Gemini colleagues like the Notorious B.I.G., Kanye West, Lauryn Hill, Prince, Ice Cube, Azealia Banks, Andre 3000, and Remy Ma. To think, write, and speak with lightning speed and agility is a necessary skill for this craft, and clearly Gemini Suns like Kendrick can rise to this occasion. Along with his contemporaries, Kendrick shares vulnerable, heartbreaking, complex, and honest lyrics about the black experience in the United States, and has been met with wide acclaim for his prose.

In his song "The Heart Part 1," Kendrick writes that he is a Gemini, and is a natural author, lover, and fighter. Not only is Kendrick accurately aware of his sun sign as being inherently creative, but he also illuminates the paradox within him. Kendrick speaks to the truth that Gemini can love hard and fight, too. These words encapsulate the tender strength, emotionality, and intelligence that Geminis can express in their lives and work beautifully. His album title, *To Pimp a Butterfly*, also touches on the Gemini transformation, as the butterfly is one of the most embodied representations of metamorphosis, and Gemini's duality is the energy that offers us all the invitation to be personal growth masterpieces in progress.

Kendrick said, "You can't categorize my music. It's human music."[8] His declaration points to the Gemini refusal to categorize—how can you do that with twin energies? Kendrick was lauded as a "master of storytelling" and his lyrics include references to racism, black empowerment, and social injustice. *Billboard* described his lyricism as "Shakespearean." Clearly Kendrick's gift for communication and his ability to reach the emotions within the shared human experience touch the hearts of people across the zodiac.

In addition to his talent in music, Kendrick performed in the Starz drama *Power* as a fast-talking Dominican named Laces, who's struggling with addiction alongside his friend 50 Cent. Letting the Gemini dissonance shine, Kendrick shared that he wanted his character to be as different from his musical persona as possible. So Kendrick drew inspiration from the people he grew up with in Compton for his episodes. Kendrick's performance was praised by critics and viewers alike.

Kendrick Lamar is one of contemporary culture's most preeminent artists. Drawing on stories and experiences that demand representation, Kendrick uses the power of the pen and his voice to expand awareness and visibility across arenas.

HARVEY MILK

The last figure we'll explore as a Gemini who expresses this archetype in the world is American politician Harvey Milk. Born in a New York City suburb on May 22, 1930 to a family of Lithuanian Jews, Harvey's life started very differently than how it ended. Harvey began his political career identifying as a conservative Republican. He was a Navy veteran, a high school teacher, and a Wall Street researcher.

However, when the counterculture movement shifted American ideologies in the late sixties and early seventies, Harvey Milk, who was then forty years old, came out as a gay man. Along with many LGBTQ+ people, Harvey migrated to the Castro District of San Francisco in 1972. Marked by the beginning of this identity-based community, Harvey's Gemini mind quickly understood the power a small but tight-knit community can have in terms of leveraging political influence. Harvey was disappointed by the lack of public services in the Castro, so he ran as a Democrat for San Francisco city supervisor in an effort to increase public funding for underserved areas, among a range of other progressive policies. Harvey lost two elections.

Not a Gemini to take defeat personally, he ran for a third time—Gemini's lucky number, as it is the third sign in the zodiac—and he was successful. In a Gemini parallel, at the time of Harvey's campaign, there was an oppositional movement to gay rights in the United States. The Briggs Initiative sought to ban anyone in the LGBTQ+ community from working as a teacher in California public schools. Harvey was a leader in the opposition against this initiative, and his Gemini skills of persuasion and inspiration garnered the support of President Jimmy Carter. The Briggs Initiative failed.

Harvey's courage, and the way he used language to name a range of emotions, from shame to authenticity, galvanized his supporters into coalitions. Harvey said, "Hope will never be silent," and one can read the Gemini message in his quote, because it inspires the reader to understand that if hope is left in silence and secrecy, it cannot survive. Without a voice, a message, and a community, hope is powerless. Harvey's comfort with visibility, emotional exposure, and risk set many in the LGBTQ+ community free from leaving their own stories in the darkness of the closest. Harvey gave hope to those who needed someone else's faith to lean on in imagining a world where one can be free to live as they authentically are without shame or judgment.

In his Gemini intelligence, Harvey must have intuited his assassination. He was killed by another city supervisor only a few months into his term. Harvey recorded three tapes in the event of his untimely death. On one of them, Harvey said, "If a bullet should enter my brain, let that bullet destroy every closet door in the country." You can connect the fact that Harvey understood the Gemini connection between the self and the collective in this reflection. His wholehearted commitment to truth telling, advocacy, and compassion on both the personal and the political levels made space for a collective movement.

Readers can attest to the Gemini transformation in Harvey's life: He stayed in the closet for forty years and fulfilled what was expected of the successful heterosexual cisgendered man. At forty, he became the man he was born to be, and demonstrated in exemplary Gemini fashion the capacity for people to consciously change when they're willing to own their story, tell it, listen to others, and inspire authentic sharing. Harvey was posthumously awarded the Presidential Medal of Freedom by President Barack Obama in 2009.

The Gemini scope of Harvey, Kendrick, Marilyn, and Laverne's lives showcases the resonance and possibility of radical self-transformation in the world. So often we believe the cultural mythology that "people never change," but Geminis consistently remind us that's all we ever do. Remember: Gemini is the very first human being in the zodiac. And the differences between the immortal and mortal twins offer the catalytic charge for Gemini to reinvent, adapt, and start again. Since the Twins are the first meeting between humans in the zodiac, but the third sign in its progression, Gemini is meant to be held in the hearts and minds of the zodiac until it ends on Pisces. So, with that in mind, astrology enthusiasts cannot stand for the counterfeit notion that people never change.

Another way to see how Gemini appears in the world is to connect the mundane choices, places, and behavior we all engage in that is ruled by Gemini. Let's start with the personal. As we have learned earlier in this book, Gemini rules our perception, thoughts, analytics, language, and listening. When anyone is engaged in those practices, they are in playing on the theme of Gemini.

In the twelve houses of the zodiac, Gemini rules the third house of siblings, short-term journeys, local and domestic travel, early learning, immediate environment, and the dynamic quest for knowledge, telepathy, and mental energy.

Countries with Gemini founding dates include Tonga, Sweden, Norway, Montenegro, Guyana, Ecuador, Wales,

Belgium, Morocco, Tunisia, Sardinia, and Iceland. Gemini cities are London, San Francisco, Nuremberg, Melbourne, Tripoli, and Plymouth. If you're a Gemini-ruled person, you'll likely find a strong soul pull to these countries and cities. You'll also feel a sense of immediate belonging if you visit them, because you are a compatible match for the frequency and culture of these places.

Now that you have a greater sense of what is ruled by Gemini, you'll be able to find its energy throughout the world. You can think of every "random" interaction with these Gemini-ruled people, places, and practices as a sign from the universe. It's the divine's way of affirming your highest Gemini energy.

CONCLUSION

After covering Gemini as child, adult, parent, in love, at work, in school, in daily life, and in the world, it is my hope that you can grasp the identity of this air sign with a bit more clarity. This sign of transformation and uncertainty often sends critics into a knee-jerk rejection without meaningful contemplation on the necessity of Gemini's traits—positive and negative.

We covered Gemini as child as highly curious, mischievous, and with quicksilver energy who wants to immediately understand and experiment with their environment. The Gemini child needs to talk their ideas out, which doesn't change as they become adults. When Geminis reach their maturation in adulthood, their social competency and relational intelligence shine. When their Mercury communication skills allow the Gemini to facilitate thoughtful dialogue and discernment, Gemini can moderate between speaker and listener. This leads the way in creating a space for connection through communication to emerge, because Gemini knows how to interface with a variety of people and help them transition from separation to union.

Naturally, these skills extend to their parenting. Gemini is both fellow troublemaker and moral authority to their offspring. Their inner child never truly grows up, since the age most thematically associated with Gemini is early adolescence. Gemini never forgets the perils or joys of youth so, on the positive side, they can be a space that allows for becoming. With a healthy mode of detachment—since Gemini, as twins, knows that not everyone is them—the Gemini parent can raise children without expecting their lives to look just like the parent's.

When it comes to partnership, I firmly believe that, like all signs, Gemini can learn to love and forge connections with the entire zodiac. Astrological consciousness has expanded beyond the binary of good versus bad compatibility, especially when it comes to Gemini's relational history, which isn't either/or but always both/and. As long as Gemini and their partner understand relational theory, how to manage the paradox of love and desire, ideas on growing together, and they use the relationship as a context for healing, they'll be two little lovebirds sitting in a tree.

Though not widely known as a "hard worker," Gemini can passionately throw themselves into their work and contribute extensively to the healing of the world. The task for the Gemini is seeing their knowledge as cumulative, as well as understanding what platforms allow for their multidimensional talents. Since Pisces is the ruler of Gemini's career sector, Gemini's mission needs to be focused on service. If a Gemini doesn't feel like they're making a difference in the lives of others, their minds or hearts won't be in their chosen vocation. When they can see how they're improving the experiences of other people through their intelligence, artistry, or any other healing modality, the Gemini will feel gainfully employed and work hard to keep it that way.

An eternal student, ruled by Mercury, Gemini is gleeful in the classroom. From lower to higher education, school offers these bright-eyed students the place to focus their mental energies. Gemini will sample, mix and match, pick up, and then drop their interests along the way, a practice that should be encouraged. Gemini shouldn't feel pressured to pick a course of study until they find the school of thought that allows them to be and do all they want. School is also the laboratory for Gemini to apply their strong social skills, and they can quickly rise to leadership positions as their campus recognizes their ability to inspire others.

When it comes to food, parts of the body, and more, Gemini can choose particular habits that enhance their life. Given Gemini's brainpower, Gemini needs to set aside an hour first thing in the morning, of uninterrupted focus, concentration, and/or a meditation exercise, so their most powerful tool is working at peak capacity throughout the rest of the day. Once every light on their mind is on, Gemini flies through life with enchantment, curiosity, a sense of humor, and the social graces that connect people to others. They just need to be careful not to do too much all at once; otherwise, they overpromise and underdeliver, which creates a difficult reputation to repair.

We explored the lives of Laverne Cox, Marilyn Monroe, Kendrick Lamar, and Harvey Milk to demonstrate how Gemini can make a mark in the world. What all four of these very different Gemini personalities share is that their lives invite others to do what so many of us are so afraid of—change. These four Geminis show how owning your story without apology inspires a level of metamorphosis and devotion from others that quickly elevates them to the status of legend. They all invite not just Geminis but the entire zodiac to break free from the situations, circumstances, and events that may mire us in too much rigidity.

After I explore anything astrological, I like to leave the reader with some ethical guidance so they can use this power responsibly. Geminis, as the sign of the Twins, are a symbol of enormous connection. Twins have a sacred bond. And this union is the key ethic for all astrology.

Now that you're more familiar with Gemini, please remember to use what you know to connect to others more deeply. High-minded astrology posits that we all incarnate to understand love more carefully and practice it more compassionately. Gemini has no more or less capability to do just that. As the sign of partnership and connection, it's the Gemini imperative to use their social intelligence and communication styles to help others feel that they're less alone. Loneliness is a public health crisis throughout the world.

Gemini is a sign very qualified to ameliorate this crisis and teach us the skills that allow us to avoid it.

The highest purpose of astrology is as a tool for relationship success. So I invite you to see it as a way for others to be as connected as the Gemini and to try to avoid any weaponizing, shaming, or seeing yourself as separate from the rest of the zodiac. Remember: The zodiac wheel is a symbol of awareness of our connection and oneness. We are each other. Gemini represents this truth, and helps the rest of the zodiac understand how the quality of our relationships affect the quality of our lives.

Thank you for immersing yourself in the quest of self-discovery and seeking answers to the questions of why we are here, what we are here to do to, and with whom. May you as a Gemini and/or the Gemini you love feel worthy and courageous in the pursuit of your or their highest expression. May your curiosity, intelligence, communication skills, and connections uplift your life and take others with you on the adventure of bringing the heavens to earth.

ENDNOTES

1. Esther Perel, "The Quality of Your Relationships Determines the Quality of Your Life" (February 12, 2019). Retrieved from https://youtu.be/LmDPAOE5V2Y.
2. Brené Brown, Rising Strong (Audio blog interview). (n.d.). Retrieved from https://open.spotify.com/episode/7ngz5mzi8FnnIXfP-wbLlLL?si=xxLgKhj3Ss64oz7OvXGkag.
3. Lao Tzu and Tom Butler-Bowdon, "Tao Te Ching," in *Tao Te Ching* (West Sussex, United Kingdom: Capstone, 2012), 29.
4. Emerson, Ralph Waldo. *Self-Reliance, and Other Essays.* Dover Publications, Incorporated, 1993.
5. Brené Brown, *The Gifts of Imperfection: Let Go of Who You Think You're Supposed to Be and Embrace Who You Are* (Center City: Hazelden Publishing, 2010.
6. Shakespeare, William, et al. *A Midsummer Night's Dream.* Simon & Schuster Paperbacks, 2016.
7. Brené Brown, *The Gifts of Imperfection: Let Go of Who You Think You're Supposed to Be and Embrace Who You Are* (Center City: Hazelden Publishing, 2010.
8. https://web.archive.org/web/20170821002757/http://youheardthatnew.com/2012/09/video-kendrick-lamar-you-really-cant-categorize-my-music-its-human-music/#.

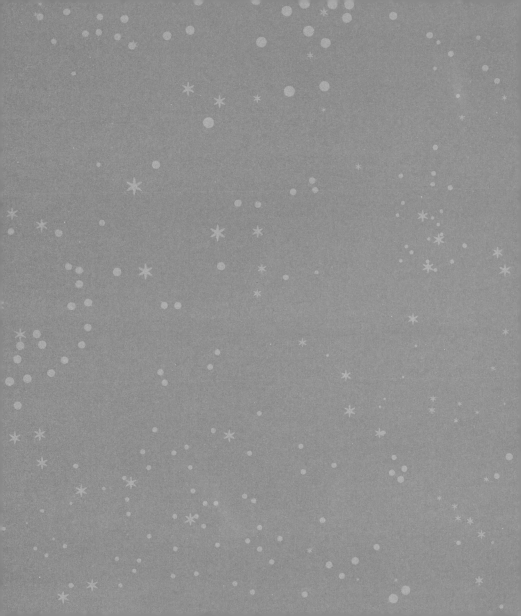

ACKNOWLEDGMENTS

Everything I do, I do for my family—my mother Kathleen, my father Brian, my brother Brendon, my twin Courtney. If we do choose our families, I chose the best one. Thank you for loving me. To my Gemini friends who inspire each word in this book, may you feel understood and loved. I'm so grateful for all my astrology mentors who've shown me that I can make a living from magic. Endless appreciation to Kate Zimmermann and the Sterling Team for making my author dreams come true: You've changed my life—thank you. And to all the Geminis who are holding my book, I am so grateful it's in your hands.

INDEX

GEMINI

ABOUT THE AUTHOR

COLIN BEDELL is a queer Gemini Twin who is from Long Island, New York. He's a passionate student of secular personal-growth systems and the universal spiritual themes explored in *A Course in Miracles*. Colin was a Provost's Scholar in the MA Fashion Studies program at Parsons School of Design, where he was the Student Speaker at the 2016 New School Commencement Ceremony. Complementing his work with QueerCosmos, Colin became the weekly horoscope writer for Cosmopolitan.com, a columnist for Astrology.com, and the Vice-President of an Astrology nonprofit group called Long Island NCGR.